まごころを

INSPIRATIONAL POETRY OF EMPEROR MEIJI

Songs From Hearts Sincere

Inspirational Poetry of Emperor Meiji

Frank Alanson Lombard, Brian Wilkes,
Shigeki Yamada, Cesar D. López.

Cover: Chikanobu, *Emperor Meiji at Asukayama Park*
Flyleaf: Title with seal of the author
Part One: Drawing of Emperor Meiji with his signature
Part Two: Photographs of Empress Dowager Shoken
Endpiece: Official seal of Emperor Meiji

This volume includes excerpts from materials that have entered public domain as well as original content.

ISBN-13: 978-1530302987
ISBN-10: 1530302986

ABOUT THE AUTHORS

Frank Alanson Lombard (1872-1925), originally of Worcester, Massachusetts, was Professor of English Literature and Education at Doshisha University, Kyoto, Japan, and Lecturer in English Literature, Imperial University, Kyoto, Japan. He translated poetry of the Meiji Emperor and Empress while striving to maintain the poetic structure of 5-7-5-7-7, known as *tanka* or *waka*. His works on Japanese drama and theater arts were also published.

Cesar D. López was born in 1986 in Maracaibo, Venezuela. He's a Physics Professor, Electronic Engineer and apprentice of Japanese language at Goen Maracaibo Academy. He works as online teacher of Spanish and Japanese.

Shigeki Yamada was born in Japan in 1952. He has been living in Venezuela for more than 40 years. He's the director of Goen Maracaibo Academy. This academy focuses in the cultural interchange between Japan and Venezuela.

Brian Wilkes is a longtime student of Asian cultures, trained in martial arts and Japanese Buddhism. During his Buddhist training, he was exposed to the concepts of Reiki, a Japanese indigenous healing art based on Buddhist and Shinto self-improvement traditions. He came to recognize the reforms of the Meiji period as central to the development and spread of Reiki. He holds a B.S. in Education, B.A. and M.A. in Ministry, an honorary doctorate from Wolsey Hall Theological College, Oxford, UK, and is a Ph.D. candidate in Ministry. He holds Shihan (Master Teacher) certificates in four lineages of Reiki, and is developing university curriculum in the discipline.

Imperial Japanese Poems of the Meiji Era
Translated from the Japanese
by Frank Alanson Lombard

FOREWORD to the 1915 Edition

A loyal nation is a ruler's praise; and no more exalted praise can be given the memory of Emperor Meiji than the loyalty of the Japanese people.

The following humble attempt at translation has been prompted by no thought that it could either add to or detract from his honor, but by a sincere desire that his personality might find wider utterance for those who are touched by that simplicity which is greatness and who may thereby be led the more to appreciate the ideals and aspirations of Japan.

In the translation of these *tanka*, selected from among many by the sovereigns of the Meiji Era, the original syllabic structure of thirty-one syllables, in lines of five, seven, five, seven, seven, though strange to the English ear, has been preserved; and rhyme, entirely lacking in the Japanese, has been for the most part disregarded as tending to detract from the essential simplicity of the verse.

Grateful acknowledgment is here rendered Mr. Yoshimatsu Yoshioka for aid in the initial translation. Professor Genzo Miwa for kindly criticism, the Honorable Iichiro Tokutomi for material used in the introductory sketch, Kitagaki Sheisho for the work of illustration, my friend and colleague. Dr. Kichiro Yuasa, for the artistic presentation of the initial poem as a cover design, and many others for that encouragement to which is due in large measure whatever success has been attained.

Frank Alanson Lombard,
Kyoto, February 11, 1915.

Introductory Sketch of Emperor Meiji

The personality of any man is that which is of most enduring interest to other men. Especially is this true when the man has occupied some high position or accomplished some great work for the world.

The years of the Meiji Era (1868-1912) brought Japan from obscurity into the fellowship of nations; and at this time, when the new era of Taisho is about to be graced by the coronation of His Imperial Majesty, Emperor Yoshihito, any effort whereby the personality of His Revered Father may be allowed further self-revelation to those of other tongue as well as to the people of Japan, is most fitting.

New Japan herself is Emperor Meiji's clearest word unto the modern world ; but other utterances of his may help to a better interpretation of this people; and with that purpose this translation of characteristic poems of the Meiji Era has been attempted.

Emperor Meiji was born in 1852, one year previous to the coming of Commodore Perry. From that time, until his accession to the throne at the age of sixteen, he lived amid the political confusion which attended the restoration of sovereignty by the Shogunate to the Crown.

Few rulers have been placed in more trying circumstances or in circumstances demanding clearer vision—firmer faith; and few, so young in years, have responded so royally to the efforts of devoted counselors. In 1871 General Saigo wrote of affairs in the Imperial Household:

"The Emperor is happiest when among attendants of the samurai class. He dislikes the influence of women at the

Court; but will stay from morning till night at his studies. He spends all his time in the study of Japanese, Chinese, and foreign books. He is attired more plainly than the nobility, and works harder than men of the middle class. — Of strong physique, he has also an indomitable will. He has decided to convene the principle officers of the government thrice a month that they may discuss affairs of state before him. The Emperor has put aside all pomp and arrogance, and cherishes most sincere friendship with his subjects."

These words, from one who knew intimately the inner life of the Court and who was influential in its shaping, are significant for they call before our imagination a youth industrious in study, simple in conduct, and sympathetic of heart, yet strong in that which constitutes authority. In the memory of those who knew him best during later years. Emperor Meiji lives as a man of such strength of will that into his presence even the Elder Statesmen did not come without trembling; and yet he tried sincerely to have them speak freely, voicing his own judgment only after mature deliberation. He would tolerate no ill-considered proposals but a frank statement advanced with loyal and sincere motives was ever welcome; and to the fact that he always spoke his heart and even engaged the Emperor in debate, Prince Ito owed the confidence he enjoyed.

It was not an easy thing to obtain the Emperor's consent to any important proposal relating to affairs of state; but, when consent had been once given, his decision never wavered; and his ministers could without hesitation devote themselves to the execution of his purpose. He was generally reserved, partly by nature and partly by intent, but never by artifice or strategy. Though those whom he most respected seldom received words of praise, he loved many of his associates deeply as is evidenced by acts of consideration and most touchingly by the words of delirium during his last illness. With all his firmness, there was a marked spirit of fairness, a complete lack of partiality so that, as Viscount Inouye used to say, he was a model Constitutional Sovereign.

His position, hemmed in by the ceremony of the Court, prevented the outward display of many of the most striking of his personal characteristics. They are evidenced in the poetic words with which he found delight and in which his heart found utterance. Simplicity, sincerity, sympathy, and faith characterized this man of industry, will, and devotion to duty. To him a little child was a great ideal; and his sympathy he strove to make world-wide. As though conscious that the circumstances of his life made it hard for him to feel with others in their misfortunes and privations, he not infrequently subjected himself to physical discomfort that his sympathy might be more genuine because founded upon experience.

His faith was truly religious; and with his superb confidence in that Divine Royalty of which he felt himself to be a part, there was a marked humility which counted himself but a channel of divine favor for the sake of the nation and its people.

✳✳✳

FOREWORD to the 2016 Edition

This volumes the result of a series of serendipitous discoveries.

While creating curriculum for university degree programs in Reiki, I studied the gyosei, or administrative poetry archived by the Meiji Shrine at Shibuya, Tokyo, Japan. More of a religious leader than modern political chief of government, in the late 19th century the emperor expressed his wishes through poetic statements more often than through direct commands. In this way, he sought to bring the audience into harmony with his own mindset, and thereby let it arise in minds of the subjects what might be expected of them.

The first generation of the discipline we know as Reiki was deeply influenced by the Meiji emperor's intention, and recitation of the imperial poetry was routinely practiced as a way for an already homogenous culture to become even more single-minded.

Emperor Meiji created over 100,000 of these poems, and the Empress Shoken about 30,000. While reviewing these for the most fitting examples, I stumbled across this 1915 compilation by the late Frank Alanson Lombard, and American professor who lived and taught in Japan. The existing copies in libraries around the US were sometimes worn and damaged, so I sought the aid of two Japanese language instructors, Shigeki Yamada and Cesar D. López, to re-create the original poetry as it was written, in a combination of *kanji* ideograms and *hiragana* phonetics, taking advantage of modern digital technology to provide you the reader with clear, legible materials. While Professor Lombard's remarkable translation maintained the meter, in a few cases his late-Edwardian style seems contrived to the modern reader. These have been updated to allow for smoother reading.

What you see before you is the fruit of that collaboration.

Brian Wilkes,
Illinois, March 2016

Developing the Sincere Heart

Shinto, the Way of the Gods, is deeply rooted in the way of Japanese life. I has even been said that all Japanese are Shinto by default, even those who claim to be Buddhist or Christian. Shinto has no founder, and no concept of religious conversion, but values for harmony with nature and virtues developed by insightful observation.

Kokoro can be translated as heart, mind, or spirit. Its ideogram, the saecond of the seal characters shown her, resembles an anatomical diagram of a heart. *Magokoro,* a contraction of *makoto no kokoro,* "heart of truth" can be translated as sincere heart, purified mind, purification and several other implications. *Magokoro* is one of the virtues the Shinto believer strives to develop, especially by association with those more accomplished (see Poem 93).

Magokoro is the first word of the first *waka* in this collection. We feel it captures the spirit of the entire publication. We hope that you will reflect on each poem with the goal of developing the sincere heart.

BW

Part One:
The Poetry of Mutsuhito, Emperor Meiji
(1852-1912)

睦
仁

まごころを
歌ひあげたる
言の葉は
ひとたびきけば
わすれざりけり

1.

Magokoro o
Utai agetaru
Kotonoha wa
Hitotabi kikeba
Wasure zari keri.

Songs from hearts sincere,
Though heard but once in passing,
Touching souls attune,
Can never be forgotten,
Or lost, however simple.

曇りなき
心のそこの
しらゝは
ことばのたまの
ひかりなりけり

2.

Kumori naki
Kokoro no soko no
Shiraruru wa
Kotoba no tama no
Hikari nari keri

Without a shadow,
Cloudless, floweth ever clear,
The light that shineth
Forth in crystalled words that make
Bright the depth of hearts sincere.

曇りなき
人のこゝろを
神はさやかに

千早ふる
さやかに
照らし見るらん

3.

Kumori naki
Hito no kokoro o
Chihaya furu
Kami wa sayaka ni
Terashi miru ran.

The God, who seeth
All things in secret hidden,
The cloudless bosom
Of man, sincere and faithful,
Will flood with light revealing.

目に見えぬ
神の心に
　通ふこそ
人の心の
　まことなりけれ

4.

Me ni mienu
Kami no kokoro ni
Kayo koso
Hito no kokoro no
Makoto nari kere.

With the unseen God,
Who seeth all secret things,
In the silence
Communes from the earth below,
The heart of the man sincere.

鬼神を
泣かするものは
世の中の
人の心の
まことなりけり

5.

Oni gami o
Nakasu ru mono wa
Yononaka no
Hito no kokoro no
Makoto nari keri.

Even to weeping,
The heart of the man sincere,
Moveth the bosoms,
Of spirits in peace on high,
Afar from the storms of earth.

さざれさえ
ゆくこゝちして
浅瀬の水の
山川の
早くもあるかな

6.

Sazare sae
Yuku kokochi shite
Yama kawa no
Asase no mizu no
Hayaku mo arukana.

How swiftly floweth
From its height, the mountain stream
The very sand-grains
Of its bed in motion seem
Swiftly flowing, flowing free.

おもふこと
ありのまにまに
　　　つらぬるが
いとまなき身の
　　なぐさめにして

7.

Omou koto
Ari no mani mani
Tsuranuru ga
Itoma naki mi no
Nagusame ni shite.

I have no leisure;
Yet 'tis sweet, the fleeting thought
From out of chaos
Into order fair to bring,
Shaping songs with feelings fraught.

言の葉の
上に匂ひて
ゆかしきは
人の心の
花にてありける

8.

Kotonoha no
Ue ni nioite
Yukashi ki wa
Hito no kokoro no
Hana ni arikeru.

The flower of the heart,
Alone by its sweet perfume
In secret distilled,
Embalmeth in fragrance rare
The words of the poet-song.

思ふこと
つくろふことも
をさなごころの
まだしらぬ
うつくしきかな

9.

Omou koto
Tsukurou koto mo
Mada shiranu
Osana kokoro no
Utsukushi ki kana.

Quickly flowing thoughts
In the garments of fashion to hide
As yet all untrained,
Than the heart of an innocent child
On earth can ought be fairer?

進みたる
世に生れたる
うないにも
むかしの事を
先づ教へなむ

10.

Susumi taru
Yo ni umare taru
Unai ni mo
Mukashi no koto o
Mazu oshie nan.

Unto the children,
Born in these progressive years
At which we wonder,
First all the tales of old,
Full of glory, should be told.

幼子の
もの書くあとを
見ても知れ
習へばならふ
しるしある世を

11.

Osanago no
Mono kaku ato o
Mite mo shire
Naraeba narau
Shirushi aru yo o.

Behold the baby,
Practicing with zealous care
His letter-writing;
And from him a lesson learn:
Effort brings its sure return.

つく杖に
すがるともよし　老人　の
千年の坂を
こえよとぞおもふ

12.

Tsuku tsue ni
Sugaru tomo yoshi
Oibito no
Chitose no saka o
Koeyo tozo omo.

The old man leaneth
On his staff;
I would that he should
Totter on, life's hill-slope o'er,
Yet a thousand seasons more.

ことそぎし
昔の家の
つくりさま
今も田舎に
のこりけるかな

13.

Kotosogishi
Mukashi no ie no
Tsukuri sama
Ima mo inaka ni
Nokori keru kana.

Within the country Hamlets,
God be praised, today
Still linger, here and
There, the simple, sweet old ways,
In homes old-fashioned.

さゝやかに
見ゆる家居も
かたつふり
ひとりすむには
こと足りぬべし

14.

Sasayaka ni
Miyuru iei mo
Katatsumuri
Hitori sumu niwa
Koto tari nubeshi.

Though small his dwelling,
Within that simple, bending dome,
The snail, contented,
Finds an ample space for home,
Scorning not his station.

今はとて
学びの道に　怠るな
ゆるしのふみを
得たるわらはべ

15.

Ima wa tote
Manabi no michi ni
Okotaru na
Yurushi no fumi o
Etaru warawabe.

All study scorning,
Think not now your tasks are done!
Your parchments given
Prove the strife is but begun,
Though today your hearts are proud.

つもりては
掃ふがかたく
なりぬべし
ちりばかりなる
ことゝおもへど

16.

Tsumorite wa
Harau ga kata ku
Narinu beshi
Chiri bakari naru
Koto to omoe do.

The dust that floateth
In the air, slow settleth down,
A weight that lifts not
From the shoulders, once so strong,
Bending now beneath their wrong.

時はかる

うつはの針の
　　ともすれば

くるひやすきは

人の世の中

17.

Toki hakaru
Utsuwa no hari no
Tomosureba
Kurui yasuki wa
Hito no yono naka.

The hands that measure
Time, perchance may feebly falter;
And man, misguided,
Err, his charted course to alter,
Taking wrong for righteousness.

世の中は
たかきいやしき
身をつくすこそ
　　ほどほどに
　　　つとめなりけれ

18.

Yononaka wa
Takaki iyashi ki
Hodo hodo ni
Mi o tsukusu koso
Tsutome nari kere.

Or high or lowly
Be thy station, 'tis thine own;
Thy best is duty
Do it then without a moan,
Thereby making life sublime.

天を恨み
人を咎むる
　　事はあらじ
我あやまちと
思ひかへさば

19.

Ten o urami
Hito o togamuru
Koto wa araji
Waga ayamachi to
Omoi kaesaba.

Resent not Heaven,
Nor on others cast the blame.
Thyself consider,
And behold the fault which springs
From the heart of secret things.

さしのぼる
朝日のごとく
爽かに
持たまほしきは
心なりけり

20.

Sashi noboru
Asahi no gotoku
Sawayaka ni
Motamahoshi ki wa
Kokoro nari keri

Like the morning sun,
In beaming brightness climbing
Up the eastern sky,
The mind of man should ever
Shine forth in cloudless splendor.

あくがる〜
人の心を
久方の
空にさそひて
たつ雲雀かな

21.

Akugaru ru
Hito no kokoro o
Hisakata no
Sora ni sasoi te
Tatsu hibari kana

High in the heavens,
Above all earth-born shadows,
Soareth the skylark,
With music sweet alluring
The hearts of longing mortals.

大空に
そびえて見ゆる
高根にも

登れば のぼる
道はありけり

22.

Ozora ni
Sobiete miyuru
Takane ni mo
Noboreba noburu
Michi wa ari keri

Even to the peaks
Of mountains that rise on high
Into the heaven,
A pathway ascends,
Alone by the chamber gained.

雪に堪へ

嵐にたへし　のちにこそ

松のくらいも

高く見えけれ

23.

Yuki ni tae
Arashi ni taeshi
Nochi ni koso
Matsu no kurai mo
Takaku miekere

The burden of snow,
The wild blast of the storm-wind,
Give dignified grace
To the pine-tree that bravely
Through the strife so long standeth.

雨だりに
くぼみし軒の
石見ても
難きわざとて
思ひ捨てめや

24.

Amadari ni
Kubomishi noki no
Ishi mite mo
Kataki waza to te
Omoisute meya

Beneath the eaves,
Where the trickling raindrops fall,
The stone is hollowed;
Seeing that, the hardest task
Appears possible at last.

おもふこと
貫かむよを
まつほどの
月日はながき
ものにぞありける

25.

Omo koto
Tsuranukan yo o
Matsuhodo no
Tsukihi wa nagaki
Mono ni zo arikeru.

Long are the years,
The days and months of waiting,
While we ever strive,
Our cherished purpose seeking
To realize completely.

いぶせしと
思ふ中にも
　　えらびなば
くすりとならむ
草もこそあれ

26.

Ibuseshi to
Omo naka ni no
Erabi naba
Kusuri to naran
Kusa mo koso are.

Amid the grasses,
That to us seem filthy weeds
By careful seeking,
Oft' o'er-shadowed by the reeds,
Healing herbs of grace are found.

白玉を
光なしとも
思ふかな
磨き足らざる
ことを忘れて

27.

Shiratama o
Hikari nashi tomo
Omo kana
Migaki tarazaru
Koto o wasurete.

The lusterless gem,
In its whiteness, despise not,
Forgetting the fact
That your hand the hard labor
Of its polish neglected.

弓矢もと
神のをさめし
国人は
事なき世にも
こころゆるすな

28.

Yumi ya mote
Kami no osameshi
Kunibito wa
Koto naki yo nimo
Kokoro yurusu na.

In peace remember
That of old the gods did rule
With bow and arrow;
And the noble arts of war
Cherish still in honor high.

身にはよし
はかずなりても
　つるぎ太刀
研きな忘れそ
大和心を

29.

Mi niwa yoshi
Hakazii nari temo
Tsurugi tachi
Toki na wasure so
Yamato kokoro o.

Though ye are girded
No more with the gleaming sword
Ready for battle,
Forget not, in idle sloth,
Yamato's keen soul to whet.

鞭うたば

紅葉の枝に　ふれぬべし

駒をひかへん

岡ごえのみち

30.

Muchi utaba
Momiji no edani
Furenu beshi
Koma o hikaen
Okagoe no michi.

Along the mountain,
Where maples skirt the pathway,
Lest whip should injure
The bending brilliant branches,
I'll curb my restless steed.

鞭うたば
紅葉の枝に
　　ふれぬべし
駒をひかへん
岡ごえのみち

31.

Kuni no tame
Ada nasu ada wa
Kudaku tomo
Itsukushimu beki
Koto na wasure so.

Brave with holy zeal,
In mortal strife desist not;
Yet, howe'er thou strike
The foe who wrongs thy country,
In wrath remember mercy.

国のため
斃れし人を
惜しむにも
おもふは親の
こころなりけり

32.

Kuni no tame
Taoreshi hito o
Oshimu nimo
Omowa oya no
Kokoro nari keri.

Whene'er I sorrow,
Thinking of our soldiers slain
In bloody battle,
In ray soul I grieve the more
For their parents weeping sore.

世と共に

かたりつたへよ

いのちをすてし

国のため

人のいさをは

33.

Yo to tomo ni
Katari tsutae yo
Kuni no tame
Inochi o suteshi
Hito no isao wa.

No lip should falter,
But to lip repeat the names
Of those who offered
Life for country's sake, that they
Here may live forever more.

はし居して
月見るほども
　　た〜かひの
にはの有様
　　思ひやりつ〜

34.

Hashi i shite
Tsuki miru hodo mo
Tatakai no
Niwa no arisama
Omoi yari tsutsu.

Looking at the moon,
I stand on my veranda;
Yet, e'en there my thoughts
Fly forth to fields of battle:
How fare my valiant soldiers?

おもほえず
夜を更かしけり
　国のため
たふれし人の
　もの語りして

35.

Omo oezu
Yo o fukashi keri
Kuni no tame
Taoreshi hito no
Monogatari shite.

Swiftly pass the hours,
While unheeding still I sit
Late into the night,
Talking of the men who died
Bravely for their country-side.

子等はみな
いくさのにはに
出ではて＼
翁やひとり
山田守るらむ

36.

Kora wa mi na
Ikusa no niwa ni
Idehate te
Okina ya hitori
Yamada moruran.

Unto the battle
Forth have the children all gone,
Forth to the battle,
While on the lonely hill-farm
Toileth the father alone.

照るにつけ
曇るにつけて
我か民草の

　　思ふかな

うへはいかにと

37.

Teru ni tsuke
Kumoru ni tsukete
Omo kana
Waga tami kusa no
Uewa ikani to.

In sunshine's brightness,
Or the gloom of cloudy days,
'My only question:
How, o'er hard or easy ways,
Fare the people, my people?

夢さめて
先つこそ思へ　いくさ人
向ひしかたの
便りいかにと

38.

Yume same te
Mazu koso omoe
Ikusa bito
Mukai shi kata no
Tayori ikanito.

Awaking from dreams,
To my mind, there first cometh
The question supreme:
Of my soldiers, what tidings
From the field of the conflict?

神垣に
涙手向けて
おがむらし

帰るをまちし
親も妻子も

39.

Kami gaki ni
Namida tamukete
Ogamurashi
Kaeru o machi shi
Oya mo tsumako mo.

To die is glory;
Yet before the soldiers' shrine,
All pale with waiting,
Low, in sacrificial tears,
Parents, wives and children kneel.

静かにも
世は治まりて
よろこびの
盃あげむ
時ぞ待たる〴

40.

Shizuka nimo
Yo wa osamari te
Yorokobi no
Sakazuki agen
Toki zo mataru ru.

I long for the time
When the earth at peace shall lie
Beneath a calm sky,
And they raise the cup of joy
Full of gladness unalloyed.

廣き世に
交りながら
いかなれば
せばきは人の
心なるらむ

41.

Hiroki yo ni
Majiwari nagara
Ikanare ba
Sebaki wa hito no
Kokoro naru ran.

Wide is the dwelling,
The dwelling in which men live,
Wide as the world's wide;
Yet narrow the hearts of men;
Alas, I but wonder why!

あさみどり
すみわたりたる　大空の
ひろきをおのが
心ともがな

42.

Asamidori
Sumiwatari tamu
Ozora no
Hiroki o onoga
Kokoro tomo gana.

Would that my human
Heart, as the cloudless heavens
Blue in their shining
Depths, through the boundless spaces,
Broad in its sympathy were.

千萬の
民と供にも
ます楽みは
あらじぞと思ふ
楽しむに

43.

Chiyorozu no
Tami to tomo nimo
Tanoshimu ni
Masu tanoshimi wa
Araji tozo omo.

Among the millions
Of my people, far and near,
To share a pleasure
Is, o'er every other joy,
One beyond all magnitude.

更くる夜の
霜ふむ人も
有るものを
火桶にのみや
より明かすべき

44 .

Fukuru yo no
Shimo fumu hito mo
Aru mono o
Hioke ni nomi ya
Yori akasubeki

Those there be who toil,
Treading the frozen midnight,
While at ease I sit
Warm through the long night-hours
Close to my brazier fire.

萩の戸の
花にやどれる
月かげは
賤が垣根も
へだてざるらん

45.

Hagi no to no
Hana ni yadoreru
Tsuki kage wa
Shizu ga kakine mo
Hedate zaruran.

The moon, that shineth
On my hedge in fragrant flower,
As brightly shineth
On the fence of rustic rails
Near some humble cottage-door.

桐火桶

かきなでながら
思ふかな

すきまおほはる

賤が伏家を

46.

Kirihioke
Kakinade nagara
Omou kana
Sukima okaru
Shizu ga fuseya o.

Warm by the brazier
Of kiri-wood I'm sitting,
Yet am I thinking —
How cold within his cottage
The poor man feels the wind blow.

久しくも
わが飼ふ駒の
　老いゆくを
惜しむは人に
　かはらざりけり

47.

Hisashiku mo
Waga kau koma no
Oi yuku o
Oshimu wa hito ni
Kawara zarikeri.

As for a subject,
Much I grieve when now I see
My trusty fav'rite
Growing old and weak of knee,
Worn in service's loyalty.

あやまちを
いさめかはして
親しむが
まことの友の
こころなりけり

48.

Ayamachi o
Isame kawashite
Shitashimu ga
Makoto no tomo no
Kokoro narikeri.

If there be error,
In gentle intimacy
Of love to counsel,
The heart of loyal friendship
Grows ever nearer, dearer.

ひらけゆく
道に出でても
心せよ
つまづくことの
ある世なりけり

49 .

Hirake yuku
Michi ni idete mo
Kokoro seyo
Tsumazuku koto no
Aru yo nari keri.

Though on the level
Well-known pathway of today
We lightly travel,
Care is needed lest we fall,
Tripped by error's hidden stone.

庭草に
水そそがせて
月をまつ
夏のゆふべは
思ふことなし

50.

Niwa kusa ni
Mizu sosogase te
Tsuki o matsu
Natsu no yube wa
Omoti koto nashi.

In summer evenings,
While I wait the rising moon,
And garden plants are
Being watered, fresh and fair,
Anxious thoughts no more molest.

しばらくは
をさな心に
かへりけり
よみならひにし
書をひらきて

51.

Shibaraku wa
Osana kokoro ni
Kaeri keri
Yomi narai nishi
Fumi o hirakite.

The books of childhood,
Which of old I used to learn,
I read today; and,
As their faded leaves I turn,
Am a boy again, a boy.

つかさ人
まかでし後の
夕まぐれ
こころしづかに
書をみるかな

52.

Tsukasa bito
Makadeshi nochi no
Yumagure
Kokoro shizuka ni
Fumi o mirukana.

Through hours of evening,
When from the busy office
Have gone the toilers,
Alone with heart of quiet
I read my volumes over.

秋の夜の
長くなるこそ
嬉しけれ

見る巻々の
数を盡して

53.

Aki no yo no
Nagaku naru koso
Ureshi kere
Miru maki maki no
Kazu o tsukushi te.

The autumn evenings,
I rejoice to notice, now
Are growing longer,
So that I my books may read,
Favorite volumes o'er and o'er.

司人

ささぐるふみは

多かれど

花見るほどの

ひまはありけり

54.

Tsukasa bito
Sasaguru fumi wa
Okaredo
Hana miru hodo no
Hima wa arikeri.

Many the papers
Officers eagerly bring,
Needing attention;
Yet my leisure still I find
Flowers to view with quiet mind.

ぬばたまの
夢にふた〲び
むすびけり
涼しかりつる
松のした水

55.

Nubatama no
Yume ni futatabi
Musubi keri
Suzushi karitsuru
Matsu no shita tsuyu.

Again in dreams, I
Dreaming drank from eager hand
The water springing
Pure from out the gleaming sand,
Shadowed cool 'neath bending pines.

そのもりや
ひとり見るらむ
昔わが
あつめし庭の
秋草の花

56.

Sono mori ya
Hitori miruran
Mukashi waga
Atsumeshi niwa no
Aki kusa no hana.

Upon the autumn
Grasses, blooming where in days
Gone by I planted
Them within my garden ways,
Lonely gard'ners, silent, gaze.

今の世に
思ひくらべて
いそのかみ
ふりにしふみを
読むぞたのしき

57.

Ima no yo ni
Omoi kurabete
Iso no kami
Furi nishi fumi o
Yomu zo tanoshiki.

I turn the mystic
Pages o'er; and joy to find,
Within their keeping,
Secrets, garnered in the past,
Opening wide the present's door.

千早ぶる

神ぞ知るらむ　民の為め

世をやすかれと　思ふ心は

58.

Chihaya buru
Kami zo shiruran
Tami no tame
Yo o yasukare to
Omo kokoro wa.

God must know my heart
That for the peace of the nations
Prayeth ever —
For the sake of the people,
For the sake of the people.

たらちねの
みおやのをしへ
年ふるま〳〵に
新玉の
身にぞしみける

59.

Tarachine no
Mioyano oshie
Aratama no
Toshi furu mamani
Mini zo shimi keru.

As I older grow,
The teachings of my parents,
Deep within my heart
And deeper ever sinking,
Impress their truth profoundly.

あしはらの
国とまさんと
青人草ぞ
思ふにも
たからなりけり

60.

Ashihara no;
Kuni tomasan to
Omou ni mo
Aohito kusa zo
Takara narikeru.

Whene'er I treasure
Seek for thee, Fair Land of Reeds,
The richest jewel
Still I find, to meet thy needs:
People burgeoning with deeds.

国をおもふ
道に二つは
　　なかりけり
いくさのにはに
　　たつもたたぬも

61.

Kuni o omou
Michi ni futatsu wa
Nakari keri
Ikusa no niwa ni
Tatsu mo tatanu mo.

The soldier fighteth
For his country on the field;
He also serveth
Who at home doth ever yield
Fruits of faithful industry.

国民は
一つ心に
守りけり
とほつみおやの
神のをしへを

62.

Kunitami wa
Hitotsu kokoro ni
Mamori keri
Totsu mioya no
Kami no oshie o.

I know full surely
That with single heart our Land
Obeyed the bidding
Clear of those High Gods who rule —
Ancient Sires of men who live.

としどしに
おもひやれども
山水を
くみてあそばむ
夏なかりけり

63.

Toshi doshi ni
Omoi yaredomo
Yama mizu o
Kumite asoban
Natsu nakari keri.

Year by year I think
Of cooling mountain streamlets
Yet when summer comes
I have no time for leisure
To draw their flowing waters.

おのがじし
つとめををへし
　　後にこそ
花のかげには
立つべかりけれ

64.

Onoga jiji
Tsutome o oeshi
Nochi ni koso
Hana no kage ni wa
Tatsu bekari kere.

Do your duty first;
Then only may you linger
In the shadow sweet
Of flowers that are shedding
For thee their balm and perfume.

波風の
静かなる日も
船人は
楫に心を
ゆるさざらなむ

65.

Nami kaze no
Shizuka naru hi mo
Funabito wa
Kaji ni kokoro o
Yurusazara nan.

The man on duty
Standing at the vessel's helm,
Must watch nor slumber,
Though the winds in zephyrs blow,
And the waves lie calm below.

世の中の
人のつかさと
なる人の
身の行ひよ
ただしからなむ

66.

Yononaka no
Hito no tsukasa to
Nam hito no
Mi no okonai yo
Tadashi kara nan.

The man who ruleth
Still should keep within his heart
A standard holy,
Set to guide the humbler folk,
Prone to follow not obey.

夏の夜も

ねざめがちにぞ

あかしける

世のためおもふ

こと多くして

67.

Natsu no yo mo
Nezame gachi ni zo
Akashi kern
Yo no tame omou
Koto okushite.

In summer, even,
Off I lie the short night through
In sleepless planning,
Burning still my study lights
While my Country's good I scan.

まつりごと
出でてきくまは
かくばかり
暑き日なりと
おもはざりしを

68.

Matsurigoto
Idete kiku ma wa
Kaku bakari
Atsuki hi nari to
Omowa zari shio.

The heat I felt not
When my mind with cares of state
Was taken wholly;
But in leisure hours of late
Prostrate, petulant I lie.

我心

およばぬ国の

よるひる神は

はてまでも

守りますらむ

69.

Waga kokoro
Oyobanu kuni no
Hate made mo
Yoru hiru kami wa
Mamori masuran.

Beyond my watch-care,
God will guard that distant spot,
In light and darkness,
Where the mind of man knows not
What of ill may be its lot.

罪あらば
朕を罪せよ
あまつ神
民はわがみの
生みし子なれば

70.

Tsumi araba
Chin o tsumi seyo
Amatsu kami
Tami wa wagami no
Umishi ko nareba.

Oh God in heaven,
If there be a deed of sin,
Thy wrath to merit,
Punish me; the people spare,
All are children of my care.

国民の
一つこころに
つかふるも
みおやの神の
みめぐみにして

71.

Kunitami no
Hitotsu kokoro ni
Tsukauru mo
Mioya no kami no
Mimegumi ni shite.

Not for grace of mine,
As one in heart they serve
Their country, but for those
Ancestors, high and holy,
Who rule benevolently.

つたへきて
国の寶と
なりにけり
ひじりのみよの
みことのりふみ

72.

Tsutaekite
Kuni no takara to
Narini keri
Hijiri no miyo no
Mikoto nori fumi.

Our fathers' precepts,
Handed down from ages past
By rulers holy,
Have become a Nation's treasure,
Held in reverence closely claspt.

むらぎもの
心をたねの
おひしげらせよ
をしへぐさ
やまとしまねに

73.

Miiragimo no
Kokoro o tane no
Oshie gusa
Oi shigeraseyo
Yamato shimane ni.

Throughout Yamato
May there grow abundantly
That wisdom-yielding
Herb which springs from secret seed,
Pregnant in the heart of man.

わがそのに
しげりあひけり
くさ木のなへも
外国の
おほしたつれば

74.

Waga sono ni
Shigeri aikeri
Totsu kuni no
Kusaki no nae mo
Oshi tatsure ba.

The roots of grasses
And of trees from foreign lands
With us shall flourish,
When with fost'ring care we tend
Daily the gardens of Japan.

目に見えぬ

神に向ひて

恥ざるは

人のこころの

まことなりけり

75.

Me ni mie nu
Kami ni mukai te
Haji zaru wa
Hito no kokoro no
Makoto nari keri.

Before the presence
Of the unseen Deity
May stand the mortal
Whose true heart's sincerity
Guardeth from all fear of shame.

うつせみの
世のためすすむ
　　いくさには
神もちからを
　　そへざらめやは

76.

Utsusemi no
Yo no tame susumu
Ikusa niwa
Kami mo chikara o
Soe zarame yawa.

God of Victory!
Thou wilt aid the army brave,
Fighting not for me,
But for mankind o'er the earth,
For the progress that shall be.

とこしへに
民やすかれと
祈るなる
我世を守れ
伊勢の大神

77.

Tokoshie ni
Tami yasukare to
Inoru naru
Waga yo o mamore
Ise no okami.

God of Ise! Hear
My lifelong supplication: —
Peace forever send
Through me unto my people,
For this my reign empowering.

Part Two:
The Poetry of Haruko, Empress Dowager Shoken
(1849–1914)

大宮の
うちにありても
暑き日を

いかなる山か
君は越ゆらむ

80.

Omiya no
Uchi ni arite mo
Atsuki hi o
Ikanaru yama ka
Kimi wa koyuran

E'en in the Palace,
Where shadows deep are lying,
Hot are the shadows;
What mountain's sun-baked path-way
Now toils my Royal Husband?

みがかずば

玉もかがみも

なにかせん

まなびの道も

かくこそありけれ

81.

Migakazuba
Tama mo kagami mo
Nani ka sen
Manabi no michi mo
Kaku koso arikere.

Unpolished lying,
Of what use are precious gems
And silver mirrors?
Still on learning's pathway steep
Toil alone brings fair increase.

磨かずば

玉の光は

出でざらむ

人の心も

かくこそあるらし

82.

Migakazu ba
Tama no hikari wa
Ide zaran
Hito no kokoro mo
Kaku koso aru rashi.

The unpolished gem
No slightest luster showeth
To prove it of worth;
The mind of man neglected
Reflects no light of wisdom.

白妙の
衣の塵は
はらへども
うきは心の
曇りなりけり

83.

Shiratae no
Koromo no chiri wa
Harae domo
Uki wa kokoro no
Kumori nari keri.

Easily we brush
The fallen dust from garments
Gleaming white and fair;
But from the mind beclouded
How hard to sweep the shadows!

とりとりに
造る髪挿の
花もあれど
匂ふ心の
うるはしきかな

84.

Tori dori ni
Tsukuru kazashi no
Hana mo aredo
Niou kokoro no
Uruwashiki kana.

Howe'er they fashion
To their slightest wish the flowers
Which deck the hair,
The fragrance of the bosom
Alone is beautiful.

過ぎたるは
及ばざりけり
かりそめの
言葉も仇に
ちらさざらなむ

85.

Sugi taru wa
Oyoba zari keri
Karisome no
Kotoba mo ada ni
Chirasa zara nan.

Gone beyond recall
Is the thing that has happened;
By thy breath let fall
Not a word that is thoughtless,
Like a leaf on the river.

人の見め
時とて心
ゆるびなく
身のおこなひを
まもりてしかな

86.

Hito no minu
Toki tote kokoro
Yurubi naku
Mino okonai o
Mamori teshi kana.

When no man seeth
Thy silent, secret doings,
Be not neglectful;
Guard then thy conduct strictly,
Respect thyself in judgment.

花の春
もみぢの秋の
さかづきも
ほとほどにこそ
酌ままほしけれ

87.

Hana no haru
Momiji no aki no
Sakazuki mo
Hodo hodo ni koso
Kuma mahoshi kere.

Drain not to its dregs
The sweet wine-cup that floweth: —
The cup of the spring
With its bloom, or of autumn
When the maple-fire gloweth.

たたかひの
かちのたよりを
きく毎に
みいくさの人の
身を思ふかな

88.

Tatakai no
Kachi no tayori o
Kiku goto ni
Mi ikusa hito no
Mi o omou kana.

Whenever I hear
The good news of victory
Attained in battle,
I think of our sailors brave,
Our soldiers at the front.

いかならむ
薬すゝめて
国のため

いたでおひくる
身をば救はむ

89.

Ikanaran
Kusuri susume te
Kuni no tame
Itade oikuru
Mi oba sukuwan.

To heal the wounded,
Who for Country's sake have born
Blows sad and grievous,
Healing gifts beyond all thought
Must be poured lavishly forth.

持つ人の
心によりて
玉ともなるは
瓦とも
黄金なりけり

90.

Motsu hito no
Kokoro ni yorite
Kawara tomo
Tama tomo naru wa
Kogaue nari keri.

That which becometh
Roof-tile or precious jewel.
As is the spirit
Having and holding it fast,
Such is the gold which men seek.

みだるべき
折をばおきて
　桜　花
まづ笑むほどを
ならひてし哉

91.

Midaru beki
Ori oba okite
Sakura bana
Mazu emu hodo o
Narai teshi kana.

Learn first how to smile,
Like the cherries that blossom
In beauty so rare,
E'er they scatter disheveled
By the storm-gusts that tear.

金剛石も磨かずば
玉の光は添はざらむ
人も学びの友により
善きに悪きに移るなり

92a.

Kongo seki mo   Migakazu ba
Tama no hikari wa   Sowazaran
Hito no manabi no   Tomo ni yori
Yoki mi ashiki ni   Utsuru nari

E'en as the precious diamond,
when left unpolished,
No gemlike luster
Showeth, its worth to token;

Nor good nor ill attaineth
the soul of mortal,
Apart from friendship's shaping,
life's crudeness broken.

時計の針の絶間なく
廻るが如く時の間も
日影惜しみて励みなば
如何なる業かならざらむ

92b.

Tokei no hari no	Taema naku
Meguru ga gotoku	Tokino ma mo
Hikage oshimi te	Hagemi naba
Ikanaru waza ka	Narazaran.

E'en as the hands of time,
in their ceaseless circles,
Moment by moment measure
unending ages;
The mind of man, in ceaseless
endeavor striving,
Will reap at last in infinite
lore its wages.

水は器に従ひて

其様様に

なりぬなり

人は交る友により

善きに悪きに移るなり

93a.

Mizu wa utsuwa ni   Shitagai te
Sono sama zama ni   Nari nunari
Hito wa majiwaru   Tomo ni yori
Yoki ni ashiki ni   Utsuru nari.

As is water in a dish,
be it square or round,
Shaped according to that form,
by that nature bound;
So is man by those with
whom keeps him company
Shaped and molded
good or ill for eternity.

おのれに優る善き友を
選び求めて
もろ共に
心の駒に鞭うちて
学びの道に進めかし

93b.

Onori ni masaru   Yoki tomo o
Erabi motome te   Morotomo ni
Kokoro no koma ni   Muchi uchite
Manabi mo michi ni   Susume kashi.

Better than thyself select
friends of noble part,
Emulate their virtue true
from a sincere heart;
Spur thy spirit's lagging steed
over wisdom's height,
Using them to strengthen thee
unto greater might.

Deeper Meanings of the Term "Reiki"

By this time, many of you reading the poetry have asked yourself, "What does any of this have to do with Reiki?" You may especially ask that if you have been trained in a version of Reiki which has become distant from Usui Sensei's practices, and which no longer stresses the cultural and spiritual context of Usui's time, including examination of Japanese language.

In Daoist cosmology, the individual person is the combination of several "souls" that unite to form a "team" entity.

Hun (魂; literally: "cloud soul") and *Po* (魄; "white 'lunar' soul") are types of souls in Chinese philosophy and traditional religion. Within this ancient soul dualism tradition, every living human has both a *hun* spiritual, ethereal, yang soul which leaves the body after death, and also a *po* corporeal, substantive, yin soul which remains with the corpse of the deceased and which gradually decays. Some controversy exists over the number of souls in a person; for instance, one of the traditions within Daoism proposes a soul structure of **san hun, qi po** 三魂七魄; that is, "three *hun* and seven *po*".

This is not unlike Cherokee tradition, reflected throughout the Southeastern nations, that sees the human being as a temporary union of an upper soul (spirit and mind), itself a union of three parts, and three or more lower or animalistic souls, that drive and animate the body.

In Hebrew, all living creatures are said to have a **nefesh** or "soul", but only humans and heavenly beings have a **ruach** or "spirit". The Early Christians used the Greek words **psyche** and **pneuma.** In ancient Egypt, there were "lower" souls that remained with the body after death, and the "higher" souls that flew up to the stars. Among the Egyptian as well as the Mayan, Incan, and Chinese aristocracy, the corpse was preserved at great expense to assure the it would not decompose, holding the lower souls in place in the body until such time as they can be rejoined with the higher soul(s), and the deceased possibly re-awakened in the flesh.

Bodily conception is a powerful event that unites these souls. When that new entity's body dies, the **Hun** or "higher soul" returns to Heaven to be reborn in another incarnation or to guide celestial events, while the **Po** or "lower soul" returns to Earth to dissolve gradually back into the elements.

However, if that unified being has achieved a state of "nirvana", it may choose not to "die" and break apart into separate fragments. In that event, the souls remain on the Earth plane and may become a source of guidance to those who come after. This is equivalent to the Buddhist concept of the Bodhisattva.

The result is 靈魂 **Ling Hun** a disembodied personal presence, sort of a benevolent haunting, a divine intervention, not a neutral impersonal form of "universal energy" like electromagnetism. **Ling,** understood as an ascended ancestral assisting spirit or ghost, is pronounced **Rei** in Japanese.

魂　　　　　魄　　　　　靈

hun　　　　　po　　　　　ling (rei)

Had you been raised in 19th century China or Japan, all of this would have been in the "cultural background noise" of the time. When Usui Sensei announced that as a result of his vision quest a luminous object struck his forehead and gave him the ability to heal and to pass that ability on to others, those who had been raised in that culture and language with him might have understood this implication when he called that phenomenon "REI KI".

Reiju or "receiving REI" was not understood as a password, "attuning" to an ambient background frequency like WiFi. It is more like requesting the sum of all of your ancestors who have become ascended Bodhisattvas (enlightened angelic beings who choose to remain on this plane to help others toward enlightenment) to intervene and bring you health and wisdom.

In the Shahaptan Way of Native American healing, we also call upon it frequently as *Wyaykihn,* a term applied to assistance from one's own deified ancestral spirits as well as the spirits of the natural world and of heaven above.

Brian Wilkes,
Shihan, Reiki no Shushigo;
Nehm Usui Reiki Ryoho Gakkai

For a free catalog of our titles, please visit
www.TuscanyGlobal.com/catalog/

Made in the USA
San Bernardino, CA
10 February 2020